University College Worcester

WR2 6AJ

The Peirson
UNIVERSITY

KT-572-696

A1029616

A note to adults ▶

This book shows children that science is everywhere, and that they can find out about the world for themselves by thinking and investigating.

You can help children by reading the book with them and asking questions. At the start of each story, talk about what the characters are saying. While children are investigating, you could ask: What is happening? What can you see? Why do you think this is happening? Is it what you expected to happen? Children should be supervised while they are doing the investigations.

Each story ends with a simple explanation of what has happened. There are ideas for follow-up activities at the back of the book, and children may also want to find out more from other books, CD-Roms or the Internet.

Text copyright © 2000 Brenda and Stuart Naylor
Illustrations copyright © 2000 Ged Mitchell

Designed by Sarah Borny
Edited by Anne Clark

The rights of Brenda and Stuart Naylor and Ged Mitchell to be identified
as the authors and artist of this work have been asserted.

First published in 2000 by Hodder Children's Books,
a division of Hodder Headline,
338 Euston Road, London NW1 3BH

All rights reserved

10 9 8 7 6 5 4 3 2 1

ISBN 0340 76440 6 Hardback
ISBN 0340 76441 4 Paperback

Printed in Hong Kong

Resource Area
507.
8
NAY

UNIVERSITY COLLEGE WORCESTER
A1029616
LIBRARY

Bungee Jumpers

and other science questions

**Brenda and
Stuart Naylor**

Illustrated by
Ged Mitchell

*Hodder
Children's
Books*

a division of Hodder Headline

Bungee Jumpers

Alex, Ben and Kim are watching Kim's brother and sister bungee jumping. They are wondering who will fall faster.

Your brother is bigger – he's going to fall more quickly!

**Rusty will help
you investigate.**

1 ▶ Make two lumps
of modelling clay or
dough. Make one big
and one small.

2 ▶ Hold one in each
hand and drop them
both at the same
time. You could ask
someone else to
drop them for you.

3 Watch when they hit the ground. Do they both land at the same time? Try it a few times.

What did you find out!

Size does not normally make a difference to how quickly something falls. Big and small things fall at the same speed and land at the same time. But things fall more slowly if their shape helps the air to slow them down.

The Bird Bath

It has been hot and sunny. Yesterday Rusty, Kim and Ben put some water in the bird bath. The water has already gone.

Perhaps the hot sun dried up the water.

Alex will help you investigate.

1 Get two saucers and put a teaspoonful of water in each.

2 Put one in a warm, sunny place.

3 ▶ Put the other in a cold, dark place.

4 ▶ See where the water lasts longer.

What did you find out?

The Sunflower

Kim, **Rusty** and Alex are trying to grow a sunflower. They are thinking about what to do to help it grow.

Plants need lots of light to make them grow.

Ben will help you investigate.

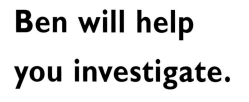

1 Find three plants which are growing in pots. You could use pots of cress.

2 Put one near a window in the light, but don't water it.

3 Give one some water, then put it in a dark cupboard.

4 Water the third one and leave it near a window in the light.

5 Leave them all for a few days and see which has grown best.

What did **you** find out?

We need food to keep us healthy and help us to grow. Plants have different food. They get their food from the light and from water.

Kim will help you investigate.

▶ You can use three ice cubes instead of ice lollies.

2 ▶ Wrap one ice cube in a layer of foil.

3 ▶ Wrap another in a layer of bubble wrap.

4 ► Wrap the third in a layer of newspaper.

5 ► Wait a while and see what happens.

What did you find out?

Heat can go easily through foil. Heat cannot go so easily through things which trap air, like bubble wrap. Something that does not let heat pass through is called an insulator.

Now you have started finding out, you might not want to stop!

Bungee Jumpers

Watch the way that things fall. Can you find some things which fall slowly, like the parachute? Try a balloon, paper, a feather or a sycamore seed. Check with a grown up before you drop anything.

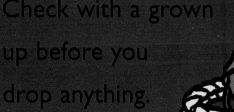

The Bird Bath

Does water dry up anywhere else? Do your hands dry when they are wet? How quickly does a puddle dry up after it has been raining? You could draw a chalk line round the edge and see what happens.

The Sunflower

Can you keep a plant growing for a long time? How much does it grow? You could measure it by putting marks on a stick. Do some plants grow taller than others? You could try marigolds, beans, tomatoes or any other plants.

Ice Lollies

How long can you keep an ice lolly wrapped in bubble wrap? Does it last longer if you use more layers? Does putting it in cold water help? Does standing in a shady place help?

Have fun finding out more!